Why Are Black Holes Black?

Thomas Canavan

ARCTURUS

This edition first published in 2014 by Arcturus Publishing

Distributed by Black Rabbit Books
P.O. Box 3263
Mankato
Minnesota MN 56002

Printed in the United States

Library of Congress Cataloging-in-Publication Data

Canavan, Thomas, 1956-
  Why are black holes black? : questions and answers about space / Thomas Canavan.
     p. cm. -- (Science FAQ)
  Audience: 4-6.
  Summary: "Answers common questions young readers have about Space"--Provided by publisher.
  Includes bibliographical references and index.
  ISBN 978-1-78212-395-8 (library binding)
  1. Astronomy--Miscellanea--Juvenile literature. 2. Outer space--Miscellanea--Juvenile literature. I.
Title.
  QB46.C27 2014
  520--dc23
                      2013004697

Editor: Joe Harris
Picture researcher: Joe Harris
Designer: Ian Winton

Picture credits: NASA: 10 bl, 20 bl, 22 c, 22 br. All other images: Shutterstock.

SL002662US
Supplier 02, Date 0414, Print Run 3559

Contents

Sunny side up

You've seen loads of sunrises and beautiful sunsets, but how much do you really know about the Sun? It's time to learn some more about your local star.

What is the Sun made out of?

The Sun is a giant ball of gas. About 70 percent of the gas is hydrogen. Most of the rest is the gas helium. The Sun has an incredibly hot core. That's where it burns hydrogen into helium. The burning releases huge amounts of energy.

How old is the Sun?

The Sun was "born" 4.6 billion years ago. It formed from a spinning ball of gas and dust. This huge ball began to spin faster and faster as it got smaller. Scientists believe that it will continue to shine for another 5 billion years. That's quite a sunny forecast!

Why does the Sun have spots?

Sunspots are parts of giant magnets inside the Sun. Our Sun has a magnetic field, but it gets twisted because the Sun spins so fast. Parts of this magnetic field pop out of the surface of the Sun. We see them as spots, and they're called sunspots. They seem dark, but that's only because they give off a little less light than the rest of the Sun.

How much energy does the Sun produce?

A family car produces about 200 horsepower. The amount of energy that the Sun produces in one second is 500,000,000,000,000,000,000,000 horsepower. That's enough to melt an ice bridge that's 2 miles (3 km) wide, 1 mile (1.6 km) thick, and goes all the way from the Earth to the Sun—in one second!

Meet the neighbors

Earth is just one of the eight planets that move around the Sun. Together they're known as the solar system. But just how much are our neighbors like us?

How did Saturn get its rings?

Those rings aren't solid like hula hoops. They're made up of many, many tiny solid objects floating around Saturn. The rings formed when the planet pulled larger objects, such as comets or even moons, toward it. Those objects crashed into each other and broke up. And the pieces are what we see as rings.

Which planets have the longest—and shortest—days?

A day is one complete turn on a planet's axis. Venus has the longest day. A "Venus day" lasts 243 "Earth days." It's even 18 "Earth days" longer than a "Venus year"! Jupiter has the shortest day. A day on Jupiter lasts just under ten hours.

Why isn't Pluto a planet anymore?

People began to wonder whether Pluto really was a planet in the late 1990s. For one thing, it turned out to be much smaller than they had thought. Astronomers (space scientists) gathered in 2005 to decide. They said that Pluto was almost a planet—but not quite. And that's because it hasn't cleared its orbit around the Sun of other objects, the way real planets do.

Could there be a planet just like Earth that's always hidden on the far side of the Sun?

People have wondered about that for many hundreds of years, but it's not the case. We can tell because of gravity. This force means that everything in space pulls on everything else. Scientists can notice that pull even if it is weak. Another planet like Earth would pull on Mercury and Venus. But no one has ever noticed any such effect.

Hey-lighten up!

Nothing moves faster than light. But the light from far-off stars still takes many years to reach us. It's time to shed some light on light—and why it means so much in our universe.

Why are **black holes** black?

Black holes form when lots of material gets squashed together. That can happen when a star collapses. Lots of material in a small space means that the force of gravity gets really strong. It's so strong that nothing can escape—not even light! And when we can't see light, an object looks black.

Does the sky seem blue on other planets?

No. We see the sky as blue because of the gases in the Earth's atmosphere. They scatter light's different colors, so we see blue. Other planets have different gases, so different colors get scattered. Mercury has no atmosphere, so the sky looks black. Venus has thick clouds and an orange sky. The sky on Mars looks red.

What are the Northern Lights?

The Earth is like a huge magnet with north and south poles. Its magnetic field protects us from dangerous electric particles that come from the Sun. The particles get pulled toward the Earth's magnetic poles. When they hit the atmosphere, they create glowing waves of light. Those colorful displays are called the Northern Lights because they can be seen in northern countries.

Why do stars twinkle?

They're not really twinkling. If you watched them from space, they would seem like steady dots of light. But we're looking at them through the gases in our atmosphere. Changing winds and heat can also change the way light seems to come through the atmosphere. The light might seem brighter for a split second, or darker. And that's what looks like twinkling.

Over the moon

We've all gazed with wonder at the full moon. But imagine how it would be to have five or six or even ten moons passing overhead each night. That's what it's like on some planets.

How far could you throw a ball on the Moon?

The Moon's gravity is six times weaker than Earth's. That means that moving objects can go six times farther. Also, the Moon has no air to slow moving objects as air does on Earth. So if you can throw a ball 100 feet (30 m) here, then on the Moon, it would go 660 feet (200 m) or more.

Is it windy on the Moon?

There's no wind on the Moon at all. That's because you need an atmosphere to create wind. It's all about gases warming up and cooling in different places. American astronauts put a U.S. flag on the Moon when they arrived in 1969. The flag was wrinkled inside a strong frame. That made it look like a flag blowing in the wind.

Do other planets have moons?

Yes. The only planets that don't have moons are the two closest to the Sun—Mercury and Venus. Mars has two moons, and scientists are constantly finding smaller moons on the outer planets. Jupiter and Saturn each have more than a dozen.

How does the Moon cause tides?

The Moon pulls on the Earth with the force of gravity. The part of Earth that's closest to the Moon gets pulled a little closer. That closest part is often the sea. We see the water rise as it's pulled slightly to the Moon. When the Moon pulls the sea closer, it's high tide. When the Earth turns and the sea is facing away from the Moon, it's low tide.

Up, up, and away

What goes up must come down. At least, that's what we expect here on Earth. Is it any different if we travel into space? It's time to find out.

What's the farthest that anything from Earth has traveled?

The United States launched the uncrewed *Voyager 1* spacecraft in 1977. Its mission was to send back information about planets in our solar system. Since then, it has sped farther and farther away from Earth. Scientists believe that it left our solar system in 2012. It is now nearly 11.2 billion miles (18 billion km) from Earth.

How much junk have humans left in space?

Bits of rockets fall back to Earth whenever something is launched into space. Some debris falls off spacecraft that are orbiting Earth. It usually stays in orbit. At least 5,000 tons of this "space junk" is circling the Earth right now.

How long would it take to fly to Mars?

A return trip to Mars would take more than a year. It would last about 420 days. That's a long time to be stuck in a spacecraft. The missions to the Moon about 40 years ago only lasted about a week each.

Could a plane travel into space if it had enough fuel?

The fuel wouldn't be the real problem. A plane wouldn't be able to fly fast enough to escape Earth's gravity. The nearest thing to a plane in space was NASA's space shuttles. They could come back to Earth and land at an airport. But they needed to get a piggyback ride on a rocket to get into space in the first place.

Here comes trouble

You've probably had to mop or sweep up after you've spilled or broken something. Would things be worse if you'd made that mistake in space—or on the Moon?

DO NOT OPEN!

Why is it a bad idea to open the door on a spacecraft?

The air inside the spacecraft has pressure (an outward push), just like air on Earth. But outside the spacecraft, there's no pressure. So the air would be pushed out into space if you opened the door. You'd get pushed out with it. Also, you'd have no air to breathe outside the spacecraft.

Which would fall faster on the Moon: a hammer or a feather?

There would be no difference. That doesn't happen on Earth because of the air. It holds some things up, such as feathers and parachutes. Other things fall quickly. On the Moon, there's no air to slow down a fall. Astronaut Buzz Aldrin took a feather and a hammer to the Moon. He dropped them—and they landed at the same time!

Could we protect Earth if an asteroid were coming straight at us?

Scientists believe that we could send a rocket to blow it up with a powerful weapon. But we would have to act quickly. The blast would blow the asteroid into thousands of pieces. These pieces could still be dangerous if the explosion was close to Earth.

What would happen if you spilled water in space?

If you were inside a spacecraft, water would float in balls. Air would be pressing in on it from all sides and holding it together. But if you were outside the ship, there would be no air pressure. The water would turn into a gas and spread apart completely.

15

Sky-high science

People have been trying to make sense of the sky above us since the earliest times. Modern tools make that search even more exciting. Let's take off on a journey of discovery.

Can scientists really listen to signals from distant stars?

Yes. When we look at stars with our naked eye or through a telescope, we are looking at light. That's a form of radiation that we can see. But stars give out lots more radiation than just visible light. They also send out radio waves. Scientists use what look like huge satellite dishes to pick up those waves. They turn the radio signals into sounds, so that they can listen to them.

How many stars can we see without a telescope?

You can see about 2,000 stars on a dark night with no Moon in the sky. You also need to be far away from city lights. Any bright light makes it harder to see faint objects such as stars in the sky.

Are astronomy and astrology the same thing?

No. Astronomy is the science related to things in the sky. Astronomers study the Sun, Moon, planets, stars—everything that's in the universe. Astrology is a belief that the stars and planets affect how people behave.

JANUARY FEBRUARY MARCH APRIL MAY JUNE JULY AUGUST SEPTEMBER OCTOBER NOVEMBER DECEMBER

What is a light year?

Quick answer—it doesn't measure time. It's a way of making it easier to understand the vast distances in space. Light travels about 186,000 miles (300,000 km) in a second. A light year is the distance that light travels in a year—around 5.88 trillion miles (9.5 trillion km).

17

Goin' my way?

When you think of space, you think of huge distances. Have you ever thought about how things in space cover those distances? Can we learn something from the way planets and comets move?

What's inside a comet's tail?

A comet is like a massive dirty snowball that travels around the Sun. The center is made of frozen water, ammonia, and other materials. They're all mixed with dust. The ice melts and turns to gas as the comet gets closer to the Sun. The gas fans out and turns into the tail that we can see.

What does it mean to be in orbit?

It means to be constantly traveling around something else. Planet Earth is in orbit around the Sun. The Moon is in orbit around the Earth. It really means that the Moon is moving forward but always being pulled toward Earth by the force of gravity. It never falls to Earth because it's heading forward. And it never flies off because it's being pulled toward Earth.

Why don't planets bump into each other?

Each of the eight planets travels around the Sun in its own orbit. The orbits become larger the farther away the planet is from the Sun. Much larger, that is—by millions of miles. That keeps the planets safely apart.

How long does it take the Sun's light to reach the edge of the solar system?

Remember that light travels at 186,000 miles (300,000 km) a second. It takes about eight minutes for the Sun's light to reach us. But it takes 16 hours for light to reach the edge of the solar system. This gives you an idea of how big our solar system is.

Tighten your space helmet

You've squeezed yourself into your spacesuit, and you're ready for takeoff. But how will you feel once the excitement wears off? Will you be the same person after a year inside that spacecraft? And is that a line for the bathroom?

How do astronauts go to the bathroom?

Their toilets look normal, but they have one big difference. Toilets on Earth use gravity to make liquids and solids land in the water. That water gets flushed away. In space, all of it would float and make a bad mess. So space toilets use air to suck liquids and solids away.

ASTRONAUTS

Who was the last person to walk on the Moon?

U.S. astronaut Eugene Cernan flew to the Moon twice. The second time was in December 1972. That was the last mission to the Moon. Cernan was the last man to get into the spacecraft heading back to Earth. He was also the last person to *drive* on the Moon. Part of his job was to drive a Moon buggy.

What is the longest anyone has ever been in space?

Valeri Polyakov spent 438 days in Russia's Mir space station in 1994–5. He broke the previous record by 74 days. Polyakov spent a long time in space to find out whether astronauts could manage a trip to Mars. Most people think that such a mission would be at least as long as Polyakov's time in space.

Do astronauts grow taller in space?

They do, because they are weightless in space. Everyone's backbone is slightly curved here on Earth. That's because of gravity pulling on us. Without that gravity, astronauts' backbones straighten out. They can gain about 2 inches (5 cm) by the end of their flight.

21

Heavens above

The night sky is much more than just a pretty background painting. It is our window to the whole universe! Remember that next time you look up on a clear night.

Why is the North Star so important?

Our spinning Earth means that the stars seem to go around in circles. We're the ones spinning, but they seem to move—except for one. The North Star is above our North Pole. Everything seems to spin around it. Sailors could always find north if they spotted that star. This allowed them to figure out their direction.

Who gets to go on the International Space Station?

This permanent space lab has been orbiting the Earth since 1998. Five space organizations have teamed up to work on it—the United States, Russia, Europe, Japan, and Canada. Each of these chooses astronauts. The organizations then meet to decide which repairs or scientific tests they need to do. Then they choose the best astronauts to match the jobs.

Did cavemen see the same constellations as us?

Yes, they saw the stars in almost exactly the same places. The patterns of constellations have looked much the same for millions of years. The stars that make them up are speeding along different paths. But to us, they hardly seem to move because they're so far away.

GANYMEDE

EUROPA

CALISTO

IO

Can we see any of the moons of other planets?

Big telescopes can see dozens of moons near other planets. But even with binoculars or a small telescope, you can see four other moons. Those all belong to the planet Jupiter. They're the first moons of another planet that anyone ever noticed. The famous Italian scientist Galileo Galilei discovered them with a homemade telescope in 1610.

23

Long ago and far away ...

When you think about the size and age of the universe, it can make you feel very small! It's hard to make sense of such large numbers.

Just what happened in the Big Bang?

Most astronomers think that the universe began in a sudden expansion (a rush of growth) that lasted much less than a second. This Big Bang happened about 14 billion years ago. It made everything that we know—matter, energy, and even time itself. The universe then cooled, and all the stars and planets formed.

How close is the nearest star, other than the Sun?

The next closest star is called Proxima Centauri. It is about 4.3 light years away. That doesn't sound so far. But that same distance works out as 25,300 billion miles (39,900 billion km).

How do planets form?

A huge spinning ball of gas turns into a star. Then pieces of that giant ball break off and form smaller balls. Those balls become planets. They continue to move in the same direction as when they broke off. But by then, they're traveling around the star in their own orbits.

What is the most distant object that we can see without a telescope?

That far-off object is the Andromeda galaxy. It contains billions and billions of stars, but we see it as a faint cloud. It's about 13 million trillion miles (21 million trillion km) away.

That's life!

Are we the only living things in the whole universe? People have wondered that since they first looked at the stars. But maybe we now have the tools to find out!

Why do people think that aliens are green?

It all began about sixty years ago. Newspapers began printing stories about people seeing aliens in "flying saucers." Several witnesses said that the flying saucers were full of "little green men." That idea stuck because it was strange and interesting.

Has anyone found life on another planet?

Not yet, but we keep trying. The best chances in our solar system are on Mars and on some of the moons of Jupiter and Saturn. Scientists are looking for traces of even the most basic life. At the same time other scientists are searching for signs of intelligent life anywhere in the universe.

Greetings from Mars!

Did scientists find signs of life on a meteorite from Mars?

In 1984, scientists found an unusual meteorite. It had begun its long journey on Mars about 16 million years ago. It seemed that something living might have made some tiny holes inside the meteorite. Some scientists remain hopeful. Others say that the holes aren't proof of life because they're too small.

Is there really a message for other forms of life on a spacecraft sent from Earth?

The United States launched the Pioneer spacecraft in 1972. The outside of it has a message for any intelligent creatures that might find it in some far-off part of space. Pictures show maps of our solar system, human beings and Pioneer's route through space.

It's out of this world

You've been out of this world and back again quite a few times in this book. And you're ready to begin exploring space on your own now. Here is some helpful information to guide you on that wonderful voyage.

What are the asteroids' names?

Many thousands of asteroids are in a band between Mars and Jupiter. The largest and brightest have names. Some are named after Greek or Roman gods, such as Ceres. Other names, such as Pasachoff, honor scientists. Most asteroids just go by codes, such as C2231.

What is a blue moon?

The Moon orbits around the Earth in just under 28 days. That's the time it takes to go from one full moon to the next. But eleven of our months are longer than that. That means that the date of the full moon gets earlier each month. We call it a blue moon when one month has two full moons. It doesn't happen often—only "once in a blue moon."

Can you get eclipses on other planets?

You'd get an eclipse if one of your planet's moons lined up between you and the Sun, or if your planet came between the Sun and a moon. Earth is special because it gets an exact solar eclipse. The Moon is much smaller than the Sun but much closer to the Earth. Amazingly, it happens to cover the Sun exactly during an eclipse.

How does GPS work?

GPS stands for "Global Positioning System." At least 24 satellites are orbiting Earth and sending down information. A car's GPS system constantly receives information from several satellites. Its computer uses that information to figure out exactly where you are—your "global position." It then compares it with where you want to be. Then it tells you how to reach your destination.

29

Glossary

air resistance the force of air pushing back against objects that are moving through it

asteroid one of the thousands of rocky objects moving around the Sun between the paths of Mars and Jupiter

astronaut a person who travels in space

atmosphere the layers of gases that wrap around the Earth

binoculars an instrument for looking at distant objects that is made of two small telescopes attached to each other

black hole a collapsed star that has a huge amount of gravity

collapse to fall or shrink together quickly

constellation a group of stars in the night sky that form a pattern or shape

core the deepest point inside something

eclipse a period when our view of one object in the sky is blocked by another object; or when one object passes through the shadow of another object

energy the name given to the ability to do work

galaxy a collection of billions of stars

GPS (Global Positioning System) a system for finding a route from one place to another. A small machine in a car (or other vehicle) gives the driver directions based on the position of satellites, using map data

gravity the force that draws objects toward each other

helium the second-lightest chemical element

horsepower a way of measuring the power of an engine—said to be the strength of one horse

hydrogen the simplest chemical element

light year the distance that light travels in one year

magnetic field an invisible area around an object that acts like a giant magnet

meteorite a piece of rock from space that lands on Earth

orbit the path that one object travels around another, for instance, the path of the Earth around the Sun

particle a tiny object, too small to see

planet a large round object that travels in orbit around a star

radiation the process of sending off waves of energy

scatter to send in every direction without any pattern

solar system a group of a star and the planets traveling around it

space shuttle a spacecraft designed to travel between the Earth and another place, such as a space station

uncrewed when talking about a vehicle: without any human beings in control

Further Reading

13 Planets: The Latest View of the Solar System by David A. Aguilar (National Geographic Children's Books, 2011)

The Alien Hunter's Handbook: How to Look for Extraterrestrial Life by Mark Brake and Colin Jack (Kingfisher, 2012)

George and the Big Bang by Lucy and Stephen Hawking (Simon & Schuster, 2012)

Seeing the Sky: 100 Projects, Activities & Explorations in Astronomy by Fred Schaaf (Dover Publications, 2012)

Space: A Visual Encyclopedia by Dorling Kindersley (Dorling Kindersley Publishing, 2010)

Web Sites

Amazing Space
http://amazing-space.stsci.edu/
Interactive features on this informative site let visitors build the Milky Way, plan a space mission, or view awesome Hubble shots of deep field objects.

Jet Propulsion Laboratory
www.jpl.nasa.gov/education/students/
An excellent resource site, NASA's Jet Propulsion Lab includes videos on how to make a science project, homework help, space and climate information, and games. With lively and thought-provoking subject matter plus amazing images and illustrations.

NASA Kids' Club
www.nasa.gov/audience/forkids/kidsclub/flash/index.html
Brought to you by the people who put astronauts on the Moon! The site has lots of practical advice about space exploration and top-level engineering.

Windows to the Universe
www.windows2universe.org
A site managed by the National Earth Science Teachers Association that subdivides into many specialist areas, with extensive information on the Sun, Earth, solar system, and space, all presented with vivid illustrations and images.

Index